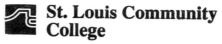

FRANCE

A Photographic Journey

TEXT: **Rupert O. Matthews**

CAPTIONS: **Fleur Robertson**

DESIGNED BY: **Teddy Hartshorn**

EDITORIAL: **Gill Waugh**

PRODUCTION: **Ruth Arthur and David Proffit**

DIRECTOR OF PRODUCTION: **Gerald Hughes**

CLB 2560
© 1991 Colour Library Books Ltd., Godalming, Surrey, England.
All rights reserved.
This 1991 edition published by Crescent Books,
distributed by Outlet Book Company, Inc., a Random House Company,
40 Engelhard Avenue, Avenel, New Jersey 07001
Printed and bound in Singapore.
ISBN 0 517 06538 X
8 7 6 5 4 3 2

FRANCE

A Photographic Journey

Text by
RUPERT MATTHEWS

CRESCENT BOOKS
NEW YORK · AVENEL, NEW JERSEY

The Gauls, the ancient people of France, exploded into history when they smashed the Roman army and went on to capture and pillage Rome in 390 BC. A century later the expansionist power of Rome ran into the Gauls again and was twice defeated: at Clusium in 295 BC and Arretium in 284 BC. Though a second sacking of Rome was avoided by a Roman victory at Lake Vadimon in 283 BC, the century of defeats was never forgotten in Rome.

With a vindictiveness typical of her foreign policy, Rome decided to destroy the power of the Gauls. By 181 BC every Gaulish tribe south of the Alps had been conquered and made subject to Rome. Even this was not enough and, in 154 BC, Rome took advantage of a plea for help from the Greek colony of Marseilles to conquer the Rhône Valley and the Languedoc. In 58 BC Julius Caesar was in need of popular support and decided to gain it by conquering the old enemy, Gaul. The areas of Gaul beyond Roman control were divided into numerous independent tribal lands, which Caesar easily conquered. But in 52 BC, an Arvenian chieftain by the name of Vercingetorix gathered a number of tribes under his leadership and revolted. Caesar laid siege to Vercingetorix's stronghold of Gergovia, but suffered such heavy casualties that he was forced to withdraw. By skilful maneuvering, however, Caesar managed to catch the Gauls at a disadvantage at Alesia, where they were crushed and Vercingetorix captured. The brave chieftain was led through the streets of Rome in chains at Caesar's triumph, and then killed.

The Gaul which Caesar had conquered was by no means a barbaric land. There was a flourishing money economy – one of the marks of civilisation – and beautiful artistic creations were common. The cultural life of the Gauls was so rich and vital that it was able largely to withstand the pressures of the Roman culture. Throughout the five centuries of Roman domination, Celtic gods continued to flourish, though under Roman names. Lug, the god of the arts, came to be identified with Mercury, so in Gaul Mercury had the attributes of Lug. A similar survival of Celtic tradition beneath a Roman veneer took place in the arts and everyday life.

Under the Romans, Gaul was divided into four provinces: *Narbonensis*, the original conquests in the south; *Aquitania*, from the Pyrenees to the Loire; *Lugdunensis*, between the Loire and the Seine, and *Belgica*, between the Seine and the Rhine. Gaul thus reached the boundaries of the Rhine, the Alps and the Pyrenees, limits which the later country of France would continually claim as her natural frontiers, but rarely achieve.

It was during the third century that various Germanic peoples began to cross the Imperial frontier and settle within Gaul. Some came as mercenaries, others as settlers on underpopulated land and still others as invaders. By the end of that century the Franks, the Germanic tribe which was to give its name to France, moved into the Empire. The same process of assimilation of cultures marked Romano-Frankish relations as had affected Gallo-Roman life four centuries earlier. It was during this period that the basics of the French character, culture and ideals were laid down. The barbarian newcomers brought fresh vitality to the declining provinces, while the indigenous population maintained its sophistication, elegance and language.

The nascent France faced its most serious threat, even as it began to take shape, when the most terrible and bloodthirsty warriors ever to invade Europe galloped into France. The Huns had already forced Constantinople to pay tribute and had destroyed numerous kingdoms, massacring whole populations in some of the most brutal conquests in history, when Attila led them into Gaul in 451. On the Catalaunian Plains the all-conquering Huns were met by a mixed force of Franks, Romano-Gauls and Visigoths and were defeated for the first and only time in their rapacious history.

The defeat of Attila marked the virtual end of the barbarian invasions, leaving the emerging France free to develop. Just thirty years later, Clovis, the first of the Merovingian kings, began the process of expansion which would make France the center of a mighty empire. Starting with a tiny holding around Tournai, Clovis embarked upon a series of brilliant military campaigns and diplomatic moves. His conversion to Roman Catholicism brought him the help of the Church against many of his enemies who adhered to the Arian heresy. By the time of his death in 511, Clovis held the whole of Gaul, except the Rhône and upper Loire valleys, and lands east of the Rhine as far as the Ems and upper Danube.

The Merovingian monarchs were soon able to push their control into Burgundy, Provence and Bavaria. Despite this success, the dynasty then began to crumble as internal family feuds, laziness and corruption dragged the Frankish Empire into bitter civil war and chaos. True power was gradually taken away from the Merovingian kings by their chief ministers, known as mayors of the palace. In 737 the Merovingian Theuderic III died and Charles Martel, mayor of the palace, seized power. Charles Martel and his son Pepin III spent their reigns reconsolidating the kingdom of the Merovingians, and it was left to Pepin's son Charlemagne to push the Frankish Empire to the limits of greatness.

Charlemagne took advantage of opportunities when they presented themselves, rather than pursuing a cohesive policy. When the Emirate of Cordoba weakened, Charlemagne pushed beyond the Pyrenees and reached the Ebro. It is with these conflicts with the Muslims that the magnificent *Chanson de Roland*, the first flowering of French literature, is concerned. Later, using the conflict between the Pope and the Lombards, Charlemagne marched into Italy and conquered the peninsula almost as far as Naples. Meanwhile, he continued his conquests in Germany, extending his control as far as the Oder, middle Danube and Dalmatia. With such massive territories under his command, and as the champion of Western Christianity, Charlemagne was able to claim the Imperial title. He was crowned as Emperor in Rome on Christmas Day 800.

The unity of the empire did not survive for long. Upon the death of Louis the Pious, son of Charlemagne, the vast territories were divided between his three heirs. The western division, which was significantly smaller than modern France, went to Charles the Bald. During the following centuries the kings were concerned with fighting off Viking raids and keeping down rebellious nobles, neither of which they did very successfully.

By the middle of the twelfth century the kings of France found themselves faced with a band of powerful nobles who resented attempts to impose royal authority. The French king was particularly unlucky in that his most powerful vassal, holding more of France than the king himself, was also king of England. Sieges, skirmishes and battles between the two kings rumbled on for decades until, in 1337, the Hundred Years' War began in earnest. Fighting raged around the English possessions in Aquitaine, Maine, Anjou and Normandy. Spectacular English successes at the battles of Crecy in 1346, Poitiers in 1356 and Agincourt in 1415 were followed by dogged resistance by the French, who steadily recaptured cities and chateaux previously lost. By the time the last English army left France in 1475 and the last Duke of Burgundy died sonless in 1477, the French kings had asserted the dominance of the royal power over too-powerful nobles.

On May 14, 1643, Louis XIV came to the throne and ushered in a new era for France. The early years of the reign, when Louis was a child, were dominated by Cardinal Mazarin, who worked ceaselessly for the good of the monarchy. Such efforts sparked off the last rebellions of the nobles, the Frondes, which were only put down with difficulty. When Mazarin died in 1661 the young king surprised everyone by taking control of the government. For the next fifty-four years Louis worked diligently for the supremacy of the monarchy and *La Gloire de La France*.

Rather than attempting to quash internal problems by force, Louis sought to neutralize the individuals. He created the most magnificent and opulent court in Europe. He built the ostentatious Palace of Versailles to house himself and his entourage and deliberately wore the most extravagant and foppish fashions. Propaganda reached fresh heights under his control as he convinced his people of his invincibility and excellence. The sheer splendor of royalty which he built up and the absolute power of the monarchy earned him the name "the Sun King", a sobriquet he encouraged by his use of a sun symbol. He made the fortunes of nobles dependent on their ability to please him personally. This brought the nobles to Versailles and forced them to adopt the fashions and rigorous etiquette upon which the king insisted. Louis then arranged for his nobles to become corrupted by gambling, decadence and scandal. The power of the nobles to oppose the monarch was thus effectively neutralized.

In his foreign policy Louis was no less determined. When the Sun King assumed the throne only France's Italian frontier had a natural boundary, and Spain owned the substantial enclave of Charolais northwest of Lyons. Mazarin negotiated a peace treaty ending a twenty-year war with Spain in 1659 which pushed the Spanish border south into the Pyrenees. It was left to Louis himself to deal with the northern and western frontiers. From 1661 onwards Louis embarked on a series of expansionist wars and diplomatic manoeuvres. By 1700 he had pushed the western frontier from around Dijon to the crest of Jura by taking the Franche-Comté from Spain. Having reached two of France's natural boundaries, the Pyrenees and the Alps, the Sun King turned to the Rhine. From Basel he pushed the frontier downstream to Lauterbourg and encroached upon the territory of the Spanish Netherlands.

In 1700 events placed all of the Sun King's achievements in peril. In that year King Charles II of Spain died heirless and left his kingdom to

Philip, Duc d'Anjou, a grandson of Louis XIV. Philip accepted the crown in order to prevent the Holy Roman Emperor putting a rival candidate on the throne and, as a result, Europe was plunged into a bitter war. Determined to prevent French expansion which had become personified in Louis XIV, Britain, the Dutch Republic and the Holy Roman Emperor formed a military alliance. The allies inflicted a series of heavy defeats upon the French at Blenheim in 1704, Ramillies in 1706 and Oudenaarde in 1708. But France continued the struggle and by 1712 the alliance had broken up and a peace was concluded which left France territorially intact.

Eighty years after the death of Louis XIV the French Revolution swept aside the monarchy, nobility and the whole apparatus of government. In their revolutionary fervor, the new government embarked upon a series of wars to spread republicanism and claimed all territory west and south of the Rhine as French. Fearful of their own position, the monarchs of Europe fell upon Revolutionary France, determined to crush her. France found her salvation in a young army officer from Corsica by the name of Napoleon Bonaparte.

In 1796 Napoleon was appointed to command the Army of Italy and proceeded to sweep across northern Italy, defeating the Austrians in the process. Success followed success for the little Corsican, and in 1799 a *coup d'état* brought Napoleon to power as First Consul of the Republic. After the Battle of Marengo in 1800, Napoleon gained recognition from the European powers of France's natural boundaries – the Pyrenees, the Alps and the Rhine – and gained immense popularity at home. By 1804 he felt popular enough to be proclaimed Emperor of France, thus ending the republic. On December 2 the Pope attended Napoleon's coronation in Notre Dame Cathedral.

Exactly one year to the day after the ceremony the new Emperor smashed the combined Austrian and Russian armies at Austerlitz. In 1806 the Prussians were beaten in the twin battles of Jena and Auerstadt and in 1807 the Russians were defeated again. Napoleon was at the height of his power. France had at last reached and surpassed her natural frontiers and owned territory around the Adriatic; Napoleon was King of Italy; his brother Joseph was King of Spain and his brother-in-law Joachim Murat was King of Naples. The west German states, known as the Confederation of the Rhine, were under French domination, as were Switzerland and the Duchy of Warsaw.

Though Napoleon instituted important reforms within France that remain in effect to this day, it is his military adventures for which he is best known. The whole Empire and its sphere of influence was built upon his military genius and the strength of the *Grande Armée*. However, when Napoleon marched half a million men into Russia in 1812 he was unwittingly undoing all his work. Less than 100,000 men returned from Moscow, and Europe turned on the defeated Emperor. He was offered France's natural boundaries but was unable to bring himself to relinquish his vast conquests. By 1814 the allies had reached Paris and Napoleon was forced to abdicate. Less than a year later, in 1815, Napoleon returned and raised a fresh army with which he defeated the Prussians at Ligny, only to meet the British under the Duke of Wellington at Waterloo three days later. The final, crushing defeat of Napoleon brought about a general redrawing of the map of Europe. At the Congress of Vienna, in 1815, the conquests of the Republic and of Napoleon were stripped from France and the monarchy restored. Though the monarchy lasted just thirty years, the boundaries of France drawn up in 1815 have lasted almost unchanged to the present day, the most significant change being the acquisition of Nice in 1860 from the Kingdom of Piedmont.

Throughout the years of expansion and contraction for France as a political entity, the nation had been developing a rich culture all its own. The early amalgam of Gauls, Romans and Franks produced, during the first millennium, the culture which is generally taken to be French. Other cultural influences, however, can be discerned within the modern nation. In the extreme northwest are the Bretons, a basically Celtic people who migrated from Britain when that country was invaded by the English some 1,500 years ago. The former Duchy only became part of France in 1532, and even then maintained local privileges. The Celtic heritage is still strong in Brittany and exerts considerable influence. Gascony has always been rather more Iberian than the rest of France and officially falls within the Pyrenean culture area. The Gascon has been traditionally thought of as impetuous by the rest of France, a role exemplified by D'Artagnan in Alexandre Dumas' novel *The Three Musketeers*. Belonging to the Mediterraneo-Alpine culture are the regions of Provence and Savoy, where the quiet hill towns are similar to their Italian counterparts across the border. Provencal literature reached a peak of excellence in the twelfth century at a time when vernacular literature in most of Europe was almost non-existent. The literature of Provence remains an important part of the area's heritage.

The aspect of French culture that has attracted most followers and imitators world-wide is its cuisine. Throughout the reigns of Clovis, Charlemagne and the Hundred Years' War French cooking had little to distinguish it from the rest of Europe. The peasants ate on a fairly basic level and the nobility were more concerned with quantity and spices. *Le Viander*, which was written around 1375 by Guillame Tirel and is the earliest important French cookbook, reveals this tendency. Bread was used to thicken soups, while cloves, ginger and nutmeg were added in quantity to disguise the putrid flavor of unrefrigerated meat.

All this was to change in 1533 when Catherine de Medici came from Florence to marry the future King Henry II. With her she brought a retinue of Italian cooks who were well versed in the delicate art of Renaissance cooking. The French learned well from the Italians and quickly adapted the Renaissance principles to their own style of cooking. In 1652 La Varenne wrote his famous work *Le Cuisinier francois* in which the basic purpose of French gastronomy was set out. He claimed that the purpose of cooking and seasoning was not to disguise flavor but to bring it out. Delicate herbs, mushrooms and truffles enhanced dishes, while roasts were actually served with their juices.

La Varenne lived during the reign of the Sun King, Louis XIV, under whose patronage the art of cooking was raised to fresh heights. Louis attached such importance to his food that the procession bringing his meals from the kitchens was escorted by two archers and the Lord Steward. At the cry "the King's meat" the corridors of the palace would be cleared to allow passage to the procession. When the splendid Palace of Versailles was built, Louis insisted on extensive kitchen gardens so that his fruit and vegetables would be truly fresh. It was under this king that the courses of a meal came to be served in a set order, rather than having all the dishes piled on the table at once. At the same time the fork replaced the fingers at mealtimes and Sèvres porcelain replaced the crude dishes and platters of earlier years.

The Revolution of 1789 affected culinary art as it affected all aspects of French life. Some great chefs were driven into exile, where they spread the excellence of French cuisine across the civilized world. Those that remained in France took to cooking in restaurants, then a new invention, bringing La Grande Cuisine to the masses. A succession of truly great French chefs over the past two centuries has kept France in the forefront of the culinary art. Names such as Carême, Escoffier and Savarin have dominated cooking with their delicate use of sauces, textures and flavorings. As well as the excellence of the great chefs of French cooking, there is a large element of tradition in the ordinary French kitchen, and some of the regions have distinctive styles. There is, however, one great culinary innovation that the French must accept as not their own. The idea of serving food individually to each diner, so that it actually arrives hot on the plate, came from Russia. Even so, it was the French who popularized the idea in the West.

An integral part of any French meal is wine. On everyday tables this may be an unassuming *vin ordinaire*, but on special occasions the truly great wines may be served. French wine is known and admired the world over for its quality and diversity. This is no accident, for the French take their wine very seriously. A central authority in Paris has representatives throughout the country who keep a close eye on wine from the better regions. If the inspectors are satisfied the wine is awarded an *Appellation Contrôlée*, which can then be displayed on the bottle. Only some fourteen per cent of French wine belongs to an Appellation Contrôlée, the strict quality control of which has played a large part in the popularity of French wine. France produces some 1,300 million gallons of wine each year, of which only some seventy million gallons are exported. With such production figures it is hardly surprising that viticulture is one of the nation's most important industries, employing almost one in ten of the working population.

Some of the most charming wines of France are those from the romantic region of the Loire. These wines are for the most part white or rosé, and are amongst the lightest and grapiest wines in the country. They do not demand the attention that a great wine needs; they may be drunk at almost any meal, enhancing the flavor of the dishes without detracting attention from them. Muscadet is found around Nantes, near the ocean, where it has its home; slightly further upstream are produced the wines of Anjou. Far upstream, beyond Orleans, are produced the wines of Sancerre and Pouilly with their peculiar smoky flavor. All the wines of the Loire are pleasant, but the northerly location means that the quality can be inconsistent. A successful practice in recent years has been to blend the less refined vintages into a wine which is ideal for the superior *méthode Champenoise* sparkling wines. The meals which accompany such delicate wines are equally subtle in flavor. The fish of the river are particularly famous, being served in such mouth-watering dishes as *brochet au beurre blanc, saumon de la Loire* and *truit au Vouvray.*

On the estuary of the Loire stands the historic city of Nantes, which was for long the capital of the Duchy of Brittany. The imposing cathedral is a fine work in the Gothic style, although it was built over a period of five centuries and is still being worked upon. The city is dominated by its ducal palace, which appears to be a medieval fortress from without, but is a Renaissance palace from within. The chateau became notorious in the fifteenth century as the home of Gilles de Rais. This rich and powerful nobleman distinguished himself in the wars with England, but in 1440 he was convicted of Satanism, heresy and the torture and murder of more than a hundred children, and was promptly executed. Further upstream is the old capital of Anjou, Angers, which stands on the Maine and is also dominated by its chateau. The Angers Chateau is purely medieval, with seventeen towers about 150-feet tall and a wide moat.

The sturdy construction of the chateau at Angers is in direct contrast to the majority of the chateaux along the Loire Valley. The beautiful climate and relaxing scenery of the valley have earned it the sobriquet of the Garden of France. The aesthetic qualities of the region were long ago realised by the kings and aristocrats of France. The region's proximity to Paris made it an ideal place for courtiers to site their country homes, while its relative isolation enabled them to get away from the court and its intrigues.

Medieval chateaux began to be converted into comfortable residences, and by the reign of Francois I the move to the Loire was well under way. It was Francois I himself who began perhaps the most magnificent of all the chateaux of the Loire. Work on Chambord started in 1519 on the site of an old hunting lodge and from its inception it was designed to outshine any humble lodge, the whole River Cosson being diverted to improve the location. An Italian architect, some claim it was Leonardo da Vinci, was brought in to design the building with its turrets, dormers and chimneys. The jumble of the roof takes on an harmonious and fairy-tale aspect when seen from afar, and the half-mile-long approach avenue emphasizes this. The chateau is set in a park which is as large as Paris and is surrounded by the longest wall in France. The 440 rooms of the chateau were ransacked during the Revolution, but they have recently been restored and the palace returned to its former splendor.

If Chambord is the most magnificent of the many chateaux in the Loire, the most romantic must be Chenonceaux. A massive medieval tower is all that remains of the original castle, which was replaced by the present elegant building. King Henry II gave the castle to his mistress, Diane de Poitiers, but after his death his wife, Catherine de Medici, evicted Diane and inhabited the castle herself. It was Catherine who extended the chateau across the river and instituted the tradition of sumptuous feasts, prepared by her Italian cooks, which would continue until the Revolution. Romance does not only belong to another age, for it is rumored that during the Second World War many wanted men were smuggled from the German-occupied north bank to the free south bank through this chateau.

The proliferation of chateaux along the valley is quite remarkable. There are so many magnificent buildings that mansions which anywhere else would be ranked as major tourist attractions are here quietly bypassed. Fifteenth-century Luynes stands solidly above its village and is now a luxury hotel. Sully-sur-Loire is another massive fortress with strong round towers and machicolations. Azay-le-Rideau, on the other hand, is the epitome of Renaissance elegance, its perfectly proportioned corner turrets and ornate gables reflecting tranquilly in the waters of the Indre.

Despite the fact that so much can be found in the countryside, it is Orleans which undoubtedly draws the attention. This city of some 100,000 people differs from the rest of the Loire in that it turns its wine into vinegar and is more concerned with industry than with agriculture. The center of the city is the beautiful cathedral which was first built in the thirteenth century, destroyed in the sixteenth and damaged again, by bombing, in the twentieth. Each time, the building was faithfully restored and is today one of the finest Gothic cathedrals in France.

To the south of the Loire is a city which was once the center of the English lands in France, but is now the center of a great wine-growing region. Even in the days of the Romans the wines of Bordeaux, then known as Burdigala, were famous and their quality has been scrupulously maintained. The University of Bordeaux has engaged in a long programme of research into what makes a good wine. They developed a theory that the major factors are weather and roots. A deep root system, it is argued, is less susceptible to floods or droughts and can therefore be relied upon to give quality wine. Vines are encouraged to produce deep roots in poor soil and, since the best Bordeaux comes from poor soils, the theory seems to work. Unfortunately it only seems true in Bordeaux.

Back in 1855 the Medoc wines, from the region north of the city, were classified according to the prices the wines had fetched over the previous century. The ten or more gradings then instituted are still in force and the various chateaux are generally ranked much as they were in 1855. In this part of France the term chateau has a quite different meaning from the chateau of the Loire. Most chateaux in Bordeaux are not grand mansions, indeed the largest building is usually the *chai,* a large, half-underground shed where wine is stored.

Despite the enthusings of wine lovers, there is a lot more to the region than wine. The city of Bordeaux itself has a population of over half a million which is engaged in a variety of industries, including recent petrochemical developments. The pride of the city is the eighteenth-century Grand Theatre, which is so elaborate that it is considered one of the wonders of the South and served as a model for many aspects of the opera house in Paris. The city was ruled by English kings for three centuries and much of the city, including the magnificent Cathedral of Saint André, dates back to that time. The Black Prince, son of the English King Edward III, ruled in Bordeaux for some years and his name is still revered.

To the east of the city is the region of the Dordogne, where the marks of man are more evocative than anywhere else in France. Thousands of years ago prehistoric man hunted mammoth and deer across the hills and valleys of the Dordogne. In most areas of the world such hunters have only left their stone tools and their bones, but in the Dordogne they have left their art. The greatest example of this prehistoric art is to be found in the cave of Lascaux, near Montignac. Dozens of horses, aurochs, deer and oxen are painted on the walls of this cavern, displaying the remarkable artistic talent which existed in the Old Stone Age. The exact purpose of the paintings has been the subject of much controversy, but experts generally agree they are ritual in nature. The Romans are represented by the arean at Périgueux and numerous other ruins throughout the area. The hills are scattered with chateaux which are far removed from the elegant chateaux on the Loire and from the wine farms of Bordeaux. The Dordogne chateaux are, for the most part, gaunt medieval strongholds perched on high, rocky peaks so as to defy attackers. Some of these crenellated fortresses reveal the Moorish influence which was once strong in the area, Castel-Bretenoux having a tower topped by an Oriental spindle.

Beyond the Garonne rise the foothills of the Pyrenees, one of the natural frontiers of France. The plains and low hills of Aquitaine are suddenly cut by the rising bulk of the mountains sparkling beneath their cover of snow. The towns and villages of the mountains are quite different from those of the rest of France, for the people belong to a different cultural stock. The ancient Romanesque churches that stand in every village seem dull from the outside, but the interiors are lavished with every treasure and masterpiece imaginable. Seven centuries ago the Albigensian heresy flourished in this region, until troops from the north descended, with Papal blessing, on the area and devastated it. Until 1589 Navarre was an independent kingdom; in that year Henry of Navarre became Henry IV of France. Such independence and a certain isolation have conspired to make the Pyreneans look upon the rest of the

French as slightly inferior beings who don't really understand.

The mountains in which these people live reach over 11,000 feet in height and are among the most scenic in Europe. Five hundred million years ago massive earth movements, known as Hercynian, created a range of mountains where the Pyrenees now stand. By 225 million years ago, however, the Hercynian mountains had been worn away and the land lay under the sea. Fresh earth movements soon broke out, more violent than before, and the present mountains were thrust upwards. During the later movements the bedrock was split in many places, and this formed hot springs which the Romans exploited as spas. After the fall of Rome the tourist potential of the mountains fell as they were fought over by Muslims, French and Spanish. It is the interest in skiing and fishing which is now bringing people back to the mountains.

Having returned to the peaks of the southwest, the French are rediscovering the peculiar cuisine of the area, which has its emphasis on garlic-enhanced stews. *Cassoulet* is a stew of pork, goose and beans which seems to vary from village to village, while the *civet d'isard* is only made from the meat of the wild goats around Pau.

There is another attraction which ensures that one town, at least, receives its share of outside visitors: Lourdes. This small town, tucked away in the western Pyrenees, is the goal of many pilgrims. In February, 1858, a young girl of the town, Bernadette Soubirous, had a vision of the Virgin Mary in the countryside nearby. The Virgin appeared a total of eighteen times to the girl, and on one occasion a spring flowed from the rock where no water was previously known. In 1862 the visions were declared authentic by Pope Pius IX and in 1933 Bernadette was declared a saint. The small town of some 17,000 citizens is dominated by its role as a pilgrimage center. Each year nearly four million pilgrims come to the town to visit the tiny Cave of the Apparitions and the enormous Basilica of Pius X. The original basilica of 1889 soon became too small for the masses of pilgrims and a new underground church of prestressed concrete was built which can hold up to 20,000 people.

Toulouse has a population of nearly half a million and is the major city of the region, with industry powered by hydro-electricity from the Pyrenees. It is the historical connections of the city which mark it out in the region. As the capital of the Visigoths it was captured by Clovis in 508, but two centuries later the Franks managed to hold it against a determined siege by the Saracens. In the anti-Albigensian campaigns Toulouse was again captured and sacked mercilessly. A third capture by force came in 1814 when the Duke of Wellington defeated Marshal Soult before the gates of the city, only to discover that Napoleon had abdicated four days earlier. Throughout its turbulent history the city has taken a special interest in architecture and has many fine buildings. The Basilica of Saint Sernin is the finest Romanesque church in the south and contains the relics of more than a hundred saints. The town's Cathedral of Saint Etienne was begun in the eleventh century, but never completed. It is from the Renaissance and sixteenth century that the bulk of Toulouse's fine buildings survive. The majestic Capitole was once the town hall and theatre and, in 1632, witnessed the execution of the Duc de Montmorency, who had unsuccessfully rebelled against the rule of Cardinal Richelieu.

Much of Toulouse's importance stems from its position on the upper Garonne. Southeast from Toulouse lies the only pass between the Pyrenees and the Massif Centrale whose gradient allows easy communications. Through this pass, from Toulouse to Carcassonne, run road, rail and canal links, all of which have had a profound effect on the development of the lands west of the Rhône. The ancient land of the

Languedoc stretches from the Spanish border the the Rhône and is bounded to the north by the Massif Centrale. Its very name emphasizes the region's individualism, for it means the "language of oc," a reference to the fact that here the word for "yes" is *oc* instead of *oui*.

Though this was the first part of Gaul to be Romanized, the Languedoc has remained little altered for centuries. The majority of the land is given over to the production of wine. Though the climate is hot and sunny, neither it nor the soil is ideal for viticulture so the wines are not the best. Paradoxically, the situation is ideal for grapes so that the wine, while low in quality, is produced in prodigious quantity. It is the inexpensive *vin ordinaire* of Languedoc which has enabled the French to drink wine in such quantity, and yet the wine brings such low prices that the Languedoc has long been one of the least-developed regions.

The capital of the Languedoc is Montpellier, which still retains its old town surrounded by broad boulevards on the site of the town walls. The winding, narrow streets are lined with elegant homes from the time of the Sun King and his successors. Beyond the boulevards a fine, modern city has spread out which has a population of a quarter of a million and engages in a variety of industries. In recent years the Languedoc has been undergoing a remarkable series of changes; industry is growing and the beaches are blossoming with hotels and resorts. The mosquito has been largely eradicated, lagoons dredged and modern hotels built with the aim of attracting holidaymakers. At La Grande Motte pyramid-shaped apartment blocks and pop-art decor combine with impressive amenities and a fine beach to produce a bustling resort quite at odds with the relaxed hinterland.

The classic holiday area of France is, of course, the Riviera, which lines the Mediterranean coast from Toulon to Menton. It is here that, in popular imagination, the sun shines brighter and the sea glitters bluer than anywhere else in Europe. In general the picture is true, though pollution and overcrowding can be a minor problem at the height of summer. Toulon has long been a major naval base for the French Mediterranean fleet, a fact which has reduced its potential as a holiday town but brought prosperity to the 200,000 inhabitants. It is said that the Roman Emperor Nero martyred a Christian named Tropes and his body was consigned to the waves. His body came ashore near a Greek colony which has ever since been known as St. Tropez. However the town gained its name, there can be little doubt that it is one of the most famous of the Riviera resorts.

Cannes lies further to the east. It first came to prominence in 1834 when Lord Brougham came here and then returned each year for more than thirty years. Many other Britons followed Lord Brougham's lead, and Cannes quickly became a favorite winter resort. Today the town is busy all year round and is popular with many other nationalities as well as the British. Still nearer to Italy is the town of Nice, which was part of Italy until 1860, when it was given to France by Piedmont for her help in defeating Austria. This large town represents for many the holiday coast, with its palm-lined Promenade des Anglais and broad beach. The town may have lost its winter status, but it has more than made up for it with a boom in summer visitors and new convention centers and casinos. Much of the town center and the old city are barred to traffic, which helps tourists unused to the reckless driving habits of the south, and ski resorts in the hills behind the town are being developed.

Set on the coast between Nice and Italy is the tiny principality of Monaco, where for years the rich have come to relax and to gamble at the famous casino. The rule of the Grimaldi family, which still reigns in

Monaco, began in 1297 and has only been interrupted by the French Revolution. The country covers less than one square mile, but in recent years has extended its area by reclaiming land from the sea. In 1962 the principality ran into a severe crisis with France because of the principality's lax taxation laws, a crisis only solved when Prince Rainier III backed down. The most famous building in the country is, of course, the casino around which the social life of Monaco revolves. The 4,000 Monégasque citizens are forbidden to gamble, but they have the consolation of not paying any income tax. They also have the distinctive food of the region in which to find solace. The proximity of Italy has replaced butter with olive oil as the main cooking medium, and bread has given way to pasta. The Mediterranean has, of course, influenced the cuisine of the region and a multitude of fish dishes are produced. Perhaps the most famous recipe from the region is *bouillabaisse*, a saffron-and-garlic-enhanced fish stew from Marseilles.

Marseilles is the great urban center of the region and the most important port and third largest city in France, having a population of one million. The port lies between the established holiday resorts of the Riviera and their growing rivals in Languedoc. The Greek colony which gave the Romans an excuse to move into Gaul is still, in many ways, an alien city on French shores. The cosmopolitan population of the port has been recently swelled by North African immigrants.

West of Marseilles the great river of southern France empties into the Mediterranean. Unlike the other major waterways of the of the country the Rhône reaches the sea across a delta some 800-square-miles in extent. This is the famous Camargue, where roam the wild, white horses and ferocious bulls which are rounded up by the French "cowboys," the *gardians*. The horses have particularly short necks and luxuriant manes and are favorites with visitors. The bulls, on the other hand, are more popular with the locals, as they are bred for the Provencal bullfights. In recent years, however, the traditionally damp landscape of the region, with its lagoons and marshes, is giving way to reclaimed land and fields as modern drainage techniques make themselves felt.

The Rhône rises six thousand feet up in the Swiss Alps, emerging from the Rhône glacier on the slopes of the Dammastock, and follows a tortuous course to the sea. On its last two-hundred-mile stretch the Rhône pours through a valley which runs between the peaks of the Alps and the bulk of the Massif Centrale. The latter is an immensely old block of rock which encompasses almost a sixth of France's total area. The majority of the region is made up of granites and schists which were thrown up during the Hercynian movements, the earliest period of upheaval which affected the Pyrenees. Unlike the mountains to the southwest, those of the Massif Centrale have lain dormant since that time and are, therefore, much lower, never reaching more than 6,200 feet. Only fairly recent volcanic activity has disturbed the ancient block, but this has built up plateaux of rock and volcanoes far larger than Italy's Vesuvius. The region has long been a less-than-affluent agricultural area, with cattle being raised on the meadows and sheep in the more barren areas. This pastoralism of the hills has resulted in the production of the cheeses for which the region is famed: Roquefort, Cantal and Bleu Saint-Nectaire.

The Alps, to the east of the Rhône, shelter pastures which also produce fine cheeses. Tomme, Sassenage and Reblochon come from the high valleys, but it is what the mountain cooks do with their cheese which marks them out from the rest of France. *Fondue savoyarde* involves melting cheese with white wine and providing bread for dunking, while *gratin dauphinois* is a delicious mixture of cheese, potatoes and cream.

Mountains which dominate the region with their ice-encrusted peaks and precipitous flanks. Winter sports enthusiasts flock here to take advantage of the snows and slopes, while in the summer the lakes of Bourget and Annecy are alive with yachts and fishermen. The greatest peak of the French Alps, indeed of Europe, is Mont Blanc. The 15,771-foot peak derives its name, which means the White Mountain, from the glaciers which cover some thirty square miles of its flanks. The first visitors came in the 1600s to gaze upon the majestic peak, but it was not until 1786 that the first successful climb was accomplished by Michel Paccard. The mountain may have been climbed, but it remained a barrier to communications until 1962, when the Mont Blanc Tunnel was completed. The tunnel links France with Italy and provides vital year-round communications between the two countries.

Between the two groups of mountains stands the city of Lyons, the second city of France. The gap cut by the Rhône through the mountains from Lake Geneva to the Mediterranean has long been an important route for communications. The city straddles the confluence of the Rhône and Saône rivers, a position which gave the impetus to its establishment as a military colony in 43 BC by the Romans. The settlement prospered and grew until it became the capital of Gaul. In AD 197 the city backed an unsuccessful claimant to the Imperial title and consequently suffered decline and fall. The Middle Ages were times of stagnation for Lyons, but the Renaissance brought revived prosperity as the silk trade dominated the city's activities. The French Revolution spelled disaster for Lyons, which was of Royalist and moderate leanings, when Republican forces took the city. Since the end of the last century textiles and chemicals have been the basis of Lyons' massive growth from a city of 400,000 inhabitants to one with a population of well over a million.

Saône, which joins the Rhône at Lyons, flows down from the north and forms an important transport route from northern France to the Mediterranean. Overlooking the valley from the foot of the Côte d'Or hills is the one-time capital of the Duchy of Burgundy: Dijon. The Burgundians were a Scandanavian people who came into the Roman Empire as mercenaries, later establishing a powerful kingdom along the Rhine. In the 430s this kingdom was destroyed by the Huns and the Burgundians were all but annihilated. The few who survived took refuge along the Saône, where they gradually rebuilt their numbers and power. By 1477 Duke Charles the Bold controlled a crescent of land from Mâcon to the North Sea and rivalled his overlord, the King of France, in power and wealth. As capital of such a powerful duchy, Dijon became a center of learning and culture. The Cathedral of Saint-Bégnigne is a magnificent example of Burgundian Gothic architecture at its best. The old Ducal Palace remains, though much altered, and contains the beautiful, fifteenth-century tombs of Duke Phillip the Bold and Duke John the Fearless. The political might of Burgundy is now gone and Dijon is perhaps best known for its mustard.

Burgundy has not lost all its greatness, however, for it ranks highly in the world of wine. Curving away southwest of the former ducal capital is an arc of hills which contains perhaps the best vineyards in France: the Côte d'Or. Between Dijon and Chagny are found some of the most famous names in wine. Nuits-St-Georges, Gevrey-Chambertin, Beaune and Meursault are all to be found in the narrow strip of land on the slopes above the Saône. Here the climate is ideal and the soil varied and rich enough to produce red wines of outstanding depth and quality with remarkable ageing properties. South of the Côte d'Or are the much larger wine produce areas of Mâcon and Beaujolais, both of which produce good, uncomplicated wine. The best of the Mâconnais is produced on the chalklands south of Mâcon and is, unlike most of the Burgundies, a white wine. Beaujolais is probably best known for the nouveau which is rushed to the world's markets within a few weeks of the crop being gathered. In the north of the region is a group of villages, the Beaujolais-Villages, which produce wine of a higher quality. Far to the north of the other regions are the vineyards around Chablis, which produce a superb white wine with as much depth and character as the Burgundy reds. The name Chablis has been copied and appropriated by so many other wine regions that almost as much "Chablis" is drunk each day as Chablis produces each year.

Another region which was of political importance centuries ago and is now in the forefront of wine production is Champagne. In 1125 Count Thibaut the Great united the area and, over the next century and a half, the County steadily grew in power and wealth. By the middle of the thirteenth century the Counts were a serious threat to the kings of France whom they alternately dominated and fought for many years. In 1284 Joan, heiress to the County, married the future Philip IV of France and decades of strife came to an end. The wealth of Champagne was to a large extent based upon the area's Fairs, which were famous throughout Christendom. Merchants came from Italy, Central Europe, England, Flanders and all over France to trade cloth, spices and precious objects at the six annual fairs, each of which lasted forty-nine days. Payment was often made in the form of a note promising payment at a later fair, and the transference of such notes marked the beginning of credit in Western Europe.

During the Hundred Years' War with England, the Champagne region was pillaged and the whole economic cycle disrupted. It was not until the seventeenth century that the prosperity of the region began to increase once more as metallurgy developed and the production of sparkling wine expanded. Champagne has become synonymous with the dry, bubbling wine and with the *méthode Champenoise* used to produce it. It is a seventeenth-century monk, Dom Pérignon, who is credited with discovering the *Méthode*, declaring as he did so, "Brothers, brothers, come quickly! I am drinking stars." The *méthode* is an intricate process which begins where most wine making methods finish. The dry white wine of the region is first fermented in the usual way and then placed in the strong bottles characteristic of Champagne, together with extra sugar and yeast. In the bottle a second fermentation takes place which raises the alcohol and carbon dioxide content of the wine. After about two years of ageing, the yeast sediment is carefully removed without losing any of the pressure which has built up within the bottle. Though the *méthode Champenoise* produces the best quality of sparkling wine, it is long and enormously expensive. Most non-Champagne sparkling wines are produced by the *cuvée close* method, which involves huge tanks of wine and the introduction of sulphur dioxide and other gases.

In the north of the Champagne is the great cathedral city of Rheims where French kings were crowned. The majestic Gothic Cathedral of Notre Dame was planned in 1211 and took a century to complete, though the towers were not added until the fifteenth century. It has a simple interior which emphasizes medieval ideas about the harmony of God, and is dominated by the deep blue rose window in the West Facade. When Clovis was baptized in an earlier church on this site in AD 496 he initiated a link between the cathedral and the monarchy which was so important that Joan of Arc made it her mission to crown the Dauphin there. After fighting numerous engagements with the English, Joan saw her King crowned at Rheims on July 17, 1429.

The northeastern corner of France has had an intricate history. The region became vital to France in her struggles with the Holy Roman Empire during the sixteenth century, when she began to encroach territorially. Lands were taken piecemeal and the region became a tangle of enclaves and exclaves, with the Duchy of Lorraine holding a patchwork of land. In 1738 Stanislaw, former King of Poland, was given the Duchy of Lorraine which, on his death in 1766, passed to his son-in-law, King Louis XV. France thus reached the approximate line of her present border in the region. But after the catastrophic defeat of Napoleon III in 1871 parts of Lorraine and Alsace were annexed by Germany, who returned them in 1919.

The cities of the area, so long independent, have maintained their individual character down to the present day and in some areas German is commonly heard. Metz was one of the cities acquired early by France when Henry II offered to defend its Protestant citizens from Catholic persecution. From 1552 onwards Metz was occupied by France, though this position was not recognized until 1648. The city is in a strategic position on road, rail and canal routes and has prospered accordingly. This position has also embroiled Metz in much fighting, most recently in 1944 when a long battle resulted in the city's liberation.

Unlike Metz, Nancy, to the south, escaped damage during the Second World War and the magnificent buildings of Stanislaw remain. These front onto the Place Stanislas and include the Hotel de Ville, a triumphal arch, and the Palais du Gouvernement, together making the finest group of eighteenth-century French buildings in existence. Until Stanislaw took over Lorraine, Nancy was two distinct walled cities, but in 1750 the separating walls were torn down and the city became one.

On the eastern border of France, near the Rhine, stands the ancient city of Strasbourg. When the Romans arrived the site was occupied by a Gallic village and has been inhabited ever since. For many years Strasbourg was a free city within the Holy Roman Empire, but in 1681 it was seized by Louis XIV and, apart from the period 1871 to 1919, it has remained within France. Despite being so far inland, Strasbourg is one of the largest grain ports in the country, being linked by canals to the Rhine, Marne and Rhône.

The territory from Lorraine to the English Channel, or *La Manche* as the French know it, has long been an invasion route both into and out of France. It was through this area that the Franks came in the fourth century AD, to be followed a century later by the Huns. The area was the scene of many of Louis XIV's greatest campaigns and was the starting point for Napoleon's *Grande Armée* when it marched to Ulm, Austerlitz and Moscow. Conversely, the region has twice this century been the scene of a full-scale invasion of France: in 1914 and 1939. There can be little wonder that successive rulers of France have tried to make the easily defended Rhine the border in this war-torn region.

Such a history of bloodshed and destruction has not stopped the area from becoming one of the major industrial centers of the nation. Transport links are especially fine in the form of railways, motorways and canals which run across an almost flat landscape, broken only by towns and slag heaps. Lille is the largest of the industrial conglomerates in the region with a population approaching 200,000. The city is the main textile center of France and also has chemical and food processing complexes. The city was taken by the armies of Louis XIV in 1667, but its proximity to the border has led to it being lost and liberated several times since then. During the seventeenth century Lille was fortified by the great French military engineer Sébastien Le Prestre de Vauban, of whose work much remains. Vauban revolutionized the art of siege warfare, both from the offensive and defensive view, building 160 fortresses for the Sun King. The slightly smaller city of Amiens to the southeast has a similar industrial make-up, but is distinguished by a waterborne market, where local farmers sell their products from small boats, and by its soaring Gothic Cathedral of Notre Dame.

West of the industrial north is a region known as the Garden of France because of its fruitfulness. During the ninth century bands of Vikings were pillaging widely across Europe, but one group of these "Northmen" settled around the mouth of the Seine. In 911 they exacted a treaty from King Charles III of France which gave them control over the territory. In time the Northmen gave their name to the lands they held, which became known as Normandy. The Normans created an efficient state governed by strong rulers which enabled them to conquer the Kingdom of England in 1066 and Sicily and southern Italy in the eleventh and twelfth centuries. As a major English possession in France, Normandy became a frequent battleground during the Hundred Years' War. The sounds of war returned to Normandy in June, 1944, when the largest invasion fleet ever assembled came from England and landed 156,000 men on the beaches of occupied France. Today Normandy is one of the most prosperous farming areas in France, even though it is not wine country. The vast orchards of apple trees, however, produce an ideal alternative to grapes, and cider is the most common local drink. More important, perhaps, is *calvados*, a type of apple brandy which features prominently at any traditional table. Land which is not used for orchards is generally given over to grazing, which results in dairy produce being a vital ingredient in local cuisine. Any dish which has the *à la normande* is almost guaranteed to involve a rich cream sauce. Camembert is probably the best known of the nearly two dozen varieties of cheese originating in Normandy and is admired throughout France as well as abroad.

Rouen has long been the center of the region both politically and economically. It stands some seventy miles inland on the Seine and yet is one of the most important ports in the country, with twelve miles of docks. The port and the proximity of the national capital have made the city into an important industrial center with more than 100,000 citizens. The crowning glory of the city is its cathedral, which exhibits a variety of medieval styles and ideas which are somehow blended together. The cathedral's bell tower is named the *Tour de Beurre* in recognition of the importance of dairy products to the region.

One of the smaller towns of Normandy, being scarcely one tenth the size of Rouen, is Bayeux. Though there are more important towns and finer cathedrals in Normandy, Bayeux is unique because of its tapestry. Strictly speaking the Bayeux tapestry is not a tapestry at all, it is a piece of embroidery, but this does not detract from its historical importance. The 230-foot-long work was probably commissioned by Odo, Bishop of Bayeux and half-brother of William the Conqueror, to commemorate the latter's conquest of England in 1066. Southwest of Bayeux, on the Golfe de St Malo, stands the Mont St Michel. This fantastic structure, perched high upon its rock, began as a simple oratory for the Bishop of Avranches in 709. Over the centuries it grew in importance and size as fortifications and ecclesiastical structures were built on the top of the rock. The mount itself is one of the natural wonders of France. It stands isolated in the center of a 100-square-mile bay which at low tide is dry land. As the tide rises, however, the sea races across the sand at a staggering yard per second, a speed which has led to more than one death in this beautiful bay.

The westernmost point of mainland France is the headland west of Brest in Brittany. As befits its remote situation Brittany has a heritage and culture which marks it out from the rest of France. Unlike most other Frenchmen, who are of mixed Romano-Gallic-Frankish stock and culture, the Bretons are Celtic. In the fifth and sixth centuries the Britons were under increasing attack from the invading English and many of them fled across the Channel to the safety of Armorica, which was then named Brittany after them. The Bretons have a truly Celtic love of mystery and legend and a great artistic bent – tendencies which can be found in Wales and Ireland. West of Vannes the unique traditions are more in evidence than to the east. In some of the smaller villages French is rarely heard, for Breton is still a living language.

The north coast of Brittany is wild and romantic, with craggy headlands and surf-pounded bays. The more sheltered inlets are lined with sandy beaches backed by pine forests, which makes them popular resorts with those not willing to trek to the Riviera. The extreme west is dominated by Brest and the rich market garden farms which surround it. Brest was for many years France's major naval port but, though still important, has been superseded by other harbors. The south coast is far removed from the rugged north. It has wide, sandy beaches and gentle coasts with fishing villages and large holiday resorts.

At the center of France – historically, politically and economically – is Paris. Paradoxically, the capital has little to do with viticulture – perhaps its only contribution in this direction is the Paris goblet, considered ideal for drinking Burgundy. Though the Franks' center of power lay to the north, Paris formed the territorial basis of the kings of France from the ninth century onwards. From Paris and the Ile de France the kings pushed out, gathering the territory of powerful vassals and taking foreign domains to increase their power and wealth.

As the center of an expanding power Paris has produced the finest buildings the country could afford. The city was founded more than two thousand years ago by the Parisii tribe on an island in the Seine. It was on that same Ile de la Cité that, in 1163, Pope Alexander III laid the foundation stone of the Cathedral of Notre Dame. Completed by 1330, but much altered since, the cathedral has become a symbol of Paris. Dominating the Place de l'Etoile is the mighty Arc de Triomphe, built to celebrate the victories of of Napoleon and the *Grande Armée*. The 164-foot-high arch is inscribed with the names of 384 campaigns and is awash with sculptures and reliefs.

The most impressive monument left by any ruler is the Palace of Versailles which lies to the southwest of the city. It was the ultimate statement of *La Gloire* which Louis XIV, the Sun King, was to build. The twenty-one years of work began in 1661 and involved thousands of laborers and thousands of horses. Marshes were drained and hills levelled in the name of royal power, but it was the building itself which dominated the area, and still does. This is one of the most magnificent and gorgeous palaces ever built – the gilding, sculpture and frescoes are unique. The power and majesty of the crown are stamped on this magnificent edifice, and so is the magnificence and style of one of Europe's great nations.

Previous page: a Picardy windmill sports a silhouette of an old man and his mule as a weathervane. Such beasts of burden were a common sight in this district for centuries right up to fifty years or so ago. Picturesquely – and appropriately – set in a cornfield, this mill's surroundings are typical of the flat, agricultural landscapes of northern France. Right: Mont-St-Michel seen from the air, whence it is possible to appreciate the extent of the mudflats that surround this dramatic outcrop of granite. The first abbey on this site was built after the Archangel Michael appeared in a vision to Aubert, Bishop of Avranches, in the eighth century. Tourists have been visiting Mont-St-Michel ever since, for centuries defying the tides that once crept across the mudflats to surround the mound. Today's visitors gain access via a road which remains above sea level, except in the event of a very high tide.

Below: late afternoon sun lights up the thin, tall houses on the quayside at Honfleur on the Atlantic coast. Honfleur, one of Normandy's most attractive ports, remains a busy working harbor and as such is relatively unspoilt. It has long been a haunt of artists. Left: cotton wool clouds mark a fresh summer day at Audierne in south Brittany. Just off Audierne lies the little Ile de Sein, whose entire male population of 600 men distinguished themselves by sailing to England in June, 1940, to fight with the Free French. Below left: Norman fishermen go down to the sea with nets.

Above: the elderly take their rest on the beach at Trouville, the oldest seaside resort in France and the premier bathing place on the Côte Fleurie of Normandy. Trouville, once a tiny fishing village, started to become fashionable during the Second Empire and today sports a casino patronised by Omar Sharif, one of the organizers of the galas staged here. Right: the famous planques in Deauville, Trouville's sister resort on the Côte Fleurie. Along these wooden walkways the rich and famous stroll, dressed in designer labels to see and be seen. Such sights have earned Deauville its rather crass nickname – "Doughville." Top right: Beg-Meil Beach in south Brittany and (above right) the beach at Arachon in Aquitaine in the height of summer.

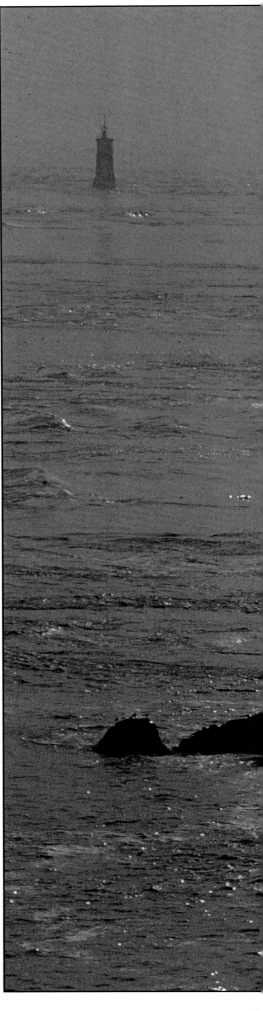

Above left: the superbly set Gothic abbey of Mont-St-Michel, which lies on the border between Brittany and Normandy. There is another reminder of the medieval outside the Calais Town Hall (left), where a bronze, The Burghers of Calais, stands. Considered one of the masterworks of the great nineteenth-century French sculptor, Auguste Rodin, this work depicts the six citizens of the town who gave themselves up as hostages to the English to save Calais in 1347. Above: a fishing boat sets a course into the sun at the end of a winter's day by the Pointe du Raz, Brittany.

During the reign of the Emperor Louis-Philippe in the mid-nineteenth century, two monumental Roman fountains (left) were built in the great space of the Place de la Concorde. This square, which lies between the Jardin des Tuileries and the Champs-Elysees, was designed to surround an equestrian statue of King Louis XIV, the Sun King; ironically, it was here that Louis XVI and his queen, Marie-Antoinette, were guillotined after the French Revolution. Today, after various additions, the square is considered to be one of the most beautiful in the world. As the statue of Louis XIV was overturned during the Revolution, its place has been filled by an Egyptian obelisk some 3,300 years old. Placed there in 1836, the obelisk is now surrounded day and night by speeding cars – a far cry from the tomb of Ramses II for which it was carved.

Top: the Basilica of the Sacré-Coeur, an eye-catching, late-nineteenth-century addition to the capital's skyline. The basilica stands in Montmartre on the highest hill in the city and is the first famous building visitors see when arriving in Paris via the Gard du Nord. Above: Notre Dame's cream-colored symmetry shimmers against a clear winter sky. One of Europe's most famous Gothic cathedrals, it was in this twelfth-century edifice that Napoleon crowned himself and here also numerous French kings and princes were married. Built on the site of a Roman temple, Notre Dame (above) dominates the Ile de la Cité, the island in the Seine that lies at the heart of Paris. Right: resplendent in gold, statues of winged horses mark the approach to the Hôtel des Invalides across Pont Alexandre III. The mortal remains of Napoleon lie in the Invalides in a tomb of red marble under the highest dome in Paris. Six outer coffins enclose a seventh in which the Emperor's body rests. It has been said, irreverently, that so many coffins were intended to ensure he did not return a third time.

Below: strolling in the Jardin des Plantes, where an avenue of trees provides a respite from the noon sun. This Parisian park boasts a small zoo, a maze and a natural history museum. Originally a herb garden for the kng's physician, the Jardin des Plantes was first opened to the public in 1650 and until 1793 was known as the Jardin du Roi. Its collections of wild and herbaceous plants are unequalled in all Paris. Left: puffing contemplatively on his pipe, an art lover pauses beside a bronze of a male nude in the tranquility of a Paris garden. Below left: a game of cards attracts attention in the Tuileries, a central Parisian park which contains the Orangerie, a fairly small museum dedicated to the works of various modern painters, includung Renoir, Cézanne, Picasso, Matisse and Rousseau, among others.

Paris by night, when nearly all the city's notable architecture is floodlit. Above left: Paris' nineteenth-century Opera House, one of the jewels of the Second Empire. This extravagant-looking building uses five different tones of marble and is bedecked with ornamental motifs and sculptures. Much of the impression it makes as one of the capital's grandest edifices is due to its position: it serves as the culmination point of the Avenue de l'Opéra, a long road which has at its other end the magnificence of the Louvre. Above: the church of Ste-Marie-Madeleine, which is one of the most famous buildings in Paris, largely owing to its site facing the Place de la Concorde. The Boulevard de la Madeleine that links the church and the square was – appropriately, perhaps – once the address of Alphonsine Duplessis, the woman upon whom Dumas based the central character of his novel, The Lady of the Camelias. *Left: lamps light the way to the Hôtel des Invalides across the Pont Alexandre III.*

Early morning light over the Place de la Concorde, an immense square, each side of which is 273 yards long. Though today this expanse is encircled only by traffic, when it was laid out in 1757 it was surrounded by a moat, a device employed to make the statue of the Sun King in the square's center look higher than it actually was. Times change, though, and just over thirty years later events took a turn that neither the Sun King, nor his architects could ever have foreseen. So many heads began to roll on the guillotine erected here during the French Revolution of 1789 that to all intents and purposes this prestigious royal place became a butcher's slab and the moat its drainage channel.

Above: one of Paris' 8,000 restaurants. This one offers food from the Alsace region near the border with Germany. Alsace cuisine has Germanic overtones, a fact indicated by the Gothic lettering on this restaurant's frontage. Left: Le Printemps, which carries an extensive selection of merchandise, including food, and is one of the major department stores of the capital. Situated near the Opera on the Boulevard Haussmann, Le Printemps comprises three buildings: the Magasin Havre, the Nouveau Magasin next door, and the Brummel in the street behind. The latter two deal in fashions for adults and children, while the former is dedicated to household goods, perfume and jewellery.

These pages: early spring in the Place du Tertre, Montmartre, where artists display their colorful oil paintings, many of which are produced in the square in the public eye. All around this square, which lies in the shadow of Sacré Coeur, are bars, cafes and restaurants where once the likes of Toulouse Lautrec, Utrillo, Picasso and Matisse might have paused to refresh themselves, since Montmartre was home to them all.

Top: a game of boules in progress under the trees of a Parisian avenue. Unlike the English game of bowls, which also involves throwing heavy balls as near as possible to a target ball, boules is meant to be played on an unsmooth surface, making it ideal as an impromptu game outside cafés on warm, lazy afternoons. Above: a Parisian takes his ease in the Bois du Boulogne amid a tangle of chairs. Right: the Rue Lagrange and the Rue Danté merge and lead towards the Pont au Double. This little bridge joins the Left Bank of Paris to the Ile de la Cité, upon which the cathedral of Notre Dame stands.

Above: the iron tracery of the Eiffel Tower is complemented by the filigree of bare branches that lines the Seine beside the Pont Alexandre III, and (above right) the Seine folds her golden arms about the Ile de la Cité as the suns sets over the capital. The Métro, the Parisian subway, is one of the fastest ways to move around the city. The first line was opened in 1900, and certain stations, notably the Bois du Boulogne entrance of Porte Dauphine and Montmartre's Abbesses (right), retain their 'art nouveau' decoration. Overleaf: fountains in the Place de la Concorde, the Eiffel Tower – the shape that represents France all over the world – in the background.

Above and top: feathers and lights and strategically placed spangles and sequins combine to present all the glamor of the Folies-Bergère, a nightclub which is world renowned for its extravagant sets, dazzling costumes, exciting sound effects and cavorting semi-nude dancers. Less expensive nights on the town in the capital can be had at one of thousands of good roadside restaurants, such as Le Consulat (left), where, on a warm evening with a good wine and a fine, albeit modest meal, people-watching can be a most relaxing pastime.

Top: the Eiffel Tower, which was a hundred years old in 1989. The Champs de Mars, the stretch of ground that lies at the foot of the tower, was the parade ground upon which Napoleon reviewed his troops. Continuing the military connection, at the end of the Champs de Mars lies the Ecole Militaire, where the officers of the French army are trained. Above: Notre Dame and (right) the Arc de Triomphe at night. The Arc was designed by Napoleon in honour of his victories and the names of 384 of his campaigns are carved in its stone. In the event, it was only completed four years before the Emperor's coffin passed under it after returning from St. Helena in 1840, Napoleon having died in exile in 1821. Today, this massive arch has grandeur that befits most solemn occasions; the tomb of the unknown soldier lies here and numerous victory parades have passed under its vaulted roof. Overleaf: a curly-headed cherub clutches a struggling fish under one of the ornate lampposts of the Pont Alexandre III, a Parisian bridge named in honor of the nineteenth-century Russian Czar.

The Palace of Versailles (these pages) lies fourteen miles southwest of Paris. Its name will forever be linked with that of the Sun King, Louis XIV, who transformed a comparatively modest château into a display of wealth and privilege unequalled in Europe – though there were many would-be imitators among the royalty of the Continent. As the primary residence of Louis XVI, the Sun King's grandson, it was from here that the unfortunate king and his queen, Marie Antoinette, were taken to Paris by the revolutionary mob. The extensive grounds at Versailles are considered masterpieces of French gardening. First laid out in the 1660s, the gardens remain today as they were then, essentially formal and geometric in appearance and immaculate in their symmetry and precision.

Right: hand-picking grapes at harvest time in the Montagne de Reims district of Champagne. In the Champagne region large wine companies, such as Moet et Chandon and Pommery, buy grapes from the growers, press them and then store the wine in their vast cellars while it is going through its fermentation processes. These companies are centered in Rheims and Epernay and their large-scale cellars have become tourist attractions – one even boasts a tour on a small train, a feasible idea since the underground galleries under Epernay, for example, stretch for sixty miles. Above: a very small-scale wine press, almost medieval in appearance, in the Champagne region.

Elaborate punts lie beside the fifteenth-century Loire Valley château, Azay-le-Rideau. So timeless is the atmosphere here that it is easy to imagine they are just where the attendants of Philippa Lesbahy left them after ferrying their mistress across the moat formed by the Indre River. Philippa was the wife of François I's treasurer, Giles Berthelot, and it was she who designed the château and oversaw its construction. Unfortunately for her, Berthelot was stealing from the royal funds and the couple were eventually obliged to flee, leaving Azay-le-Rideau to the king whose money had financed it. Overleaf: the magnificent Château de Chambord, which is set in a national game reserve near Blois reputed to be as large as Paris.

Above left: the Loire Valley's Château d'Amboise, where the French king Charles VIII died, rather bathetically, after hitting his head on a low doorway. In 1560 this beautiful country house was the scene of a gruesome massacre, following the discovery of a plot to abduct François I. The bodies of a thousand Protestant victims were hung around the building. On a more civilized note, it was in the town of Amboise that Leonardo da Vinci spent his last four years under the patronage of François I. Left: the château at Rigny-Ussé, where the fairytale writer Charles Perrault was thought to have been inspired to write Sleeping Beauty of the Woods. *Above: the magical setting of the Château de Chenonceaux, a mansion originally built by Henri II for his mistress, Diane de Poitiers. Upon the King's death, his wife, Catherine de Medici, took the château for herself, ousting the incumbent and forcing her to live at Chaumont, another Loire château.*

Left: bottling wine by hand and (below left) picking grapes by the bucket load near Turckheim (below) in Alsace. This town produces some of the best wine of the region. In Alsace and Lorraine, it is the custom to call wines by the name of the grape used in their making – Riesling, Traminer and Sylvaner – rather than by the vineyard or region from which they hail. The better wines, though, are denoted by area as well and Turckheim is a name to remember in this context. Overleaf: an immaculate vineyard in Vouvray, a village in the Loire valley dedicated to wine. The great white wines of Vouvray are world famous for their quality and variety; they can vary from being bone-dry to richly sweet, according to the grower and the vintage.

Above left: the small village of La Roque-Gageac, which lies in the river valley of the Dordogne. Huddled close to a high cliff face, its feet almost in the water, this is reputed to be one of the most beautiful villages in France. Left: a Dordogne château, at its most romantic during the fall, and (above) an aerial view of Limoges, a town in the Dordogne famous for its porcelain. Its Musée National Adrien-Dubouché contains the largest collection of porcelain in the world, displaying china that once belonged to personages as varied as President Ulysses S. Grant, the last Shah of Iran, Napoleon I and Queen Elizabeth II. Limoges also boasts an old quarter known as La Boucherie, which comprises narrow, winding streets and medieval buildings which still house the butchers' shops that gave the district its name in the Middle Ages.

Above: the Valentré Bridge at Cahors, one of the rare fortified stone bridges in Europe, built in the fourteenth century and financed by the merchants of this prosperous town. Situated in the Lot valley, Cahors lies on a bend in the Lot River and can also boast a fourteenth-century guard tower and a fortified and double-domed eleventh-century cathedral, St-Etienne. Above right: Château de Mavaleix in Périgord, and (right) and the eighteenth-century facade of Brântome Abbey on the banks of the Dronne at Brantôme in the Dordogne. The abbey was founded by Charlemagne in 769 and has a timeless atmosphere; the biographer Maurois called Brântome "a dream world."

Left: making Armagnac brandy in the county of the same name in Languedoc. Armagnac is a sweeter version of cognac sometimes referred to as "bottled sunshine" of which the locals are very proud – asking for cognac, rather than Armagnac, is likely to give offence in this district. Below left: a chef stands before his raw ingredients in a restaurant in Auch near the Pyrenées. Auch is the birthplace of d'Artagnan, Louis XIV's most famous musketeer, who was later immortalized in Alexandre Dumas' novel. A statue of him stands in the town square. Below: ducks and geese reared for the production of foie gras, a delicacy of the Dordogne region that involves the force-feeding of the birds in order to enlarge their livers, from which this very rich paté is made.

These pages: the lace bonnets, collars and umbrellas of the ladies combine to add a light touch to the heavy black clothes worn by the men during the Felibree, a summer festival instituted in the nineteenth century in the town of Eymet. Eymet, which lies on the River Dropt in Dordogne, devotes three months of the year to organizing this festival, making miles of garlands and over a hundred thousand paper flowers with which to decorate the streets and alleyways of the town. The festivities, which conclude with a giant banquet for over 1,200 people, are in honour of the land, the ancestral tongue of the region and the home. Overleaf: fishing boats at low tide in the harbor of St-Jean-de-Luz in the Basque county. Sailors from this town were the first to fish the Grand Banks off Newfoundland in 1520, and today the harbor is the center of the French tuna industry.

The old fortified cathedral of Saint-Nazaire on the Orb River in Béziers, which lies just nine miles from the Mediterranean in southern France. The cathedral was built in the thirteenth and fourteenth centuries but the town dates back much further than that: Béziers boasts the remains of an arena built by the Roman colony of Betarrae. It was the Romans who are thought to have introduced muscat wine to the region; the town later grew rich by trading in this wine and a museum of the history of wine can be found in Béziers. Once the stronghold of the viscounts of Carcassonne, Béziers was also the scene of a dreadful massacre in 1209, when Simon de Montfort was ordered by the Pope to rid the town of its Catharist heretics and so proceeded to murder the inhabitants. A canal separates the old town from the modern city, which has become an important railway junction.

Above: the white ponies and black bulls of the Camargue, a region of salt marsh and shallow lagoons in southern France. There are many herds of such ponies and bulls in this delta land, as well as flamingoes, egrets and numerous species of rare plants, and they are all protected in an area around Vaccarés that has been set aside as a regional park. Above left: the Hérault Gorge near St-Guilhem-le-Désert, Hérault, a little village whose tenth-century abbey church sold its cloister to the Metropolitan Museum in New York. Left: the magnificent medieval walled town of Carcassonne, Auch, the only one of its kind in Europe. Eighty per cent of the original fortifications – two sets of walls – are still in existence and it is in this that Carcassonne is unique. The two walls were impregnable – if enemy soldiers succeeded in climbing over the first, they found themselves trapped between that and the second and at the mercy of the town's defenders.

These pages and overleaf: the Mediterranean port of Marseille, which is the second largest harbor complex in Europe. Much of the Old Port was destroyed by the Nazis during the Second World War, but there are still early Christian crypts under the abbey of St-Victor, while the Foreign Legion base of St-Nicholas dates from the fifth century. Marseilles also has a variety of specialist museums, devoted to, for example, sculpture, ceramics and musical instruments. Nevertheless, it is not history or museums that first spring to mind here. Marseilles has a cosmopolitan reputation; it has been called the crossroads of a thousand races, the gateway to the Orient and the meeting place of the world. As the oldest port in France and the greatest in the Mediterranean, Marseille well deserves its reputation.

Cannes (left and above) is known throughout the world as one of the loveliest resorts on the Mediterranean. It was 'discovered' by Lord Brougham in 1834 when it was simply a tiny fishing village. The English Lord Chancellor was forced to stay overnight in Cannes after an outbreak of cholera in Nice prevented him from continuing on to that resort. He was enchanted with the surroundings and built a house in the village, to which he returned every winter for the rest of his life. Such an important person soon made the place fashionable; the English and Russian beau monde were to be seen there in considerable numbers as the century wore on. Above left: a flower-decked float in the Nice Mardi Gras Carnival, a winter affair that is Nice's best known event.

The harbor at Menton, which lies to the east of Nice very close to the Italian border. This town, formerly a fishing village, was the home of a considerable British colony before the First World War, and Winston Churchill spent numerous holidays at Roquebrune, a village close by. Today Menton is known for two festivals, a chamber music festival held in high summer and the Festival of Lemons in February. Menton is traditionally thought to be the warmest spot on the French Riviera and, encouraged by the climate, lemon trees grow in profusion in and around the town. It seems that they are nearly always either in blossom or in fruit and the festival uses hundreds of thousands of them in colorful and imaginative displays.

These pages: sun worshippers on the French Riviera – not a tan line in sight. Topless and even bottomless sunbathing is accepted here – indeed, virtually all the beaches along the Côte d'Azur are topless now, a trend that gained fashionable appeal after the film And God Created Woman... *a 1956 French film, based in St-Tropez, in which Brigitte Bardot sunbathed in the nude.*

102

Although the port at St-Tropez (these pages) was blown up in 1944 during the Second World War, one would hardly guess today, since the houses that surrounded the waterfront have all been reconstructed in the traditional shape and painted typical Mediterranean pastel shades. St-Tropez was named after a Christian called Torpetius, who was executed by the Roman emperor Nero in Pisa during the first century AD. His body was set adrift in a boat with a dog and a cock to feed on it, but, miraculously, when it came ashore months later at St-Tropez, it was neither eaten nor corrupted. The locals have considered this event worthy of celebration ever since, and each spring a replica of the corpse is carried round the town in a boat, accompanied by volleys of firearms.

These pages: the young and uninhibited set for which St-Tropez is famed. The best-known beaches, where most of the posing goes on, are some miles from the center of town: the plage de Pampelonne is reputed to have the most sand, the plage des Salins the most space, while the really wealthy flock to the plage de Tahiti. On them all, undressing, supposedly in order to sunbathe, is a guarantee that your figure will be critically assessed – St-Tropez is not for the wallflowers of the world.

These pages: Villefranche-sur-Mer, a port which lies between Mont Boron and Cap Ferrat on the French Riviera close to Nice. Situated beside a deep harbor, an asset worth defending, the town boasts a sixteenth-century fortress built by the Duke of Savoy, although Villefranche's origins as a port go back to the arrival of the Saracens in the early fourteenth century. A number of artists, including Aldous Huxley and Katharine Mansfield, have been attracted to the picturesque, narrow streets and the sheltered, forested slopes of the town and Villefranche has shown confidence in them. The writer and painter Jean Cocteau was asked to decorate the entire interior of the town's fourteenth-century Chapel of St. Pierre, which he did with bold, colorful paintings of the Apostles. Overleaf: Cassis, a small fishing port dominated by Europe's highest cliff, Cap Canaille, which rises to 1,200 feet.

Above left: St-Raphaël, a small coastal resort billed as the gateway to the Côte d'Azur. Lying only a dozen miles east of Marseille, the town's fine sand beaches are popular among weekenders from the city. Left: La Grande-Motte, a new resort on the Languedoc-Roussillon coast which boasts a lagoon for up to 1,000 pleasure craft and some startling architecture. Above: more traditional waterfront designs crowd around one of the world's most glittering harbors at Monte Carlo, perhaps Europe's best known gambling center and luxury Mediterranean resort. The capital of the sovereign state of Monaco, Monte Carlo was made even more fashionable in the fifties when the American film star Grace Kelly married Prince Ranier, later to be Ranier III and the ruler of the smallest state in the world after the Vatican. Her arrival added a touch of royal glamor to Monte Carlo that nowhere else on the Riviera could match. Overleaf: the Royal Palace of Monaco, where the Prince and late Princess lived.

Above: swathed in cloud, a peak of the Massif du Pelvoux retains its snow even in summer in the Hautes-Alpes. The French Alps are the skiing center of the country, and they also offer some of the finest scenery on the Continent. Right: the Isère River, which rises amid a collection of glaciers in the Savoy Alps on the Italian frontier and rushes down past the famous ski resort of Val d'Isère on its 180-mile-long journey to Grenoble and ultimate confluence with the Rhône.

Left: Val d'Isère, Savoie, where it is possible to ski even in midsummer – the most serious of skiers can be catered for here. All round this high-altitude resort are ski runs and cable cars to the best peaks, with trails that go up to 12,300 feet. Val d'Isère gains a certain cachet as the hometown of the French skiing star Jean Claude Killy and is widely held to be one of Europe's most exclusive ski towns. Below left: the lake formed by damming the Isère River at Tignes, a ski resort which lies just below Val d'Isère in Savoie. The dam is the highest in Europe. Below: skiers pick their way down a gentle slope in the Dauphinois region, where their swirling paths have left characteristic dimples in the snow as if a thousand icicles had dripped from on high over the mountains.

Above: the Aiguille du Midi, the destination of reputedly the highest and most spectacular cable car in the world. The scale is initially difficult to grasp, since at first glance the station appears as a bottle of wine balanced upon a small outcrop of rock – only closer inspection reveals the minute forms of skiers wending their way from the summit of Mont Midi. Mont Blanc, close by, is visible during the ride from South Chamonix, but it is not long before the car disappears into the clouds to emerge some 12,000 feet up the mountain. From the Aiguille du Midi it is possible to descend in another cable car to the village of Entrèves in Italy. Facing page: skiers brave the cold in Samoëns, a ski resort lying north of Annecy and boasting one of the best alpine gardens in France.

Below: net curtains and battlements, an incongruous combination in an imposing château overlooking a vineyard in the Rhone Valley, and (remaining pictures) Chatel-le-Berzé, one of the most beautifully situated châteaux in Burgundy. Lying south of Cluny, the château overlooks the steep slopes and outcrops of the Bois Clair Pass in a region famous for its red wine.

Above: the Cathedral of St. Jean, which overlooks the Saone River and is visible from the eighteenth-century Place Bellecour in the heart of Lyons. This, the second largest city in France, was once well-known for its trade in silk. Today it is an industrial center for mechanical and chemical firms, but the visitor will also find a well-preserved old town which boasts some superb Renaissance architecture, especially in the vicinity of the Place Bellecour. Above left: Roquefort, a famous French cheese made from ewes's milk and ripened for three months in the limestone caves of Les Causses in south-central France. The process, which has been used for thousands of years, produces a wonderfully aromatic dessert cheese. Left: some of the 264 other varieties of cheese that France can claim as her own, and for which she is envied throughout the gastronomic world.

Below: fields of vines in the Champagne region, which can boast 27,000 acres of chalkland devoted to viticulture. These vineyards, lying about 100 miles east of Paris, are some of the most northerly in the world. They are at their loveliest in the fall, when they are due to be harvested (left and below left). The region's principal grape-producing districts are the Montagne de Rheims in the north, where the Pinot Noir, a black grape, is grown; the Vallée de la Marne and the Côte des Blancs south of Epernay, where the white grape Chardonnay is cultivated. Overleaf: the owner of the Château de Saule uses a wall to advertize his residence, which is set amid a tranquil sea of vines near Lyons. Last page: winter vineyards in Burgundy.